PRAISE FOR *SLOWS: TWICE*

'T. Liem is one of my favourite poets working in Canada. I welcomed this book into my life like sudden sunlight. *Slows: Twice* is a book about how urgently we need to read differently. I loved its mischievous relation to form and expectation as well as its burning intelligence. I once described T. as an inheritor of the tradition of Language Poetry, but what *Slows: Twice* proves is that T. is less an inheritor and more so an innovator, an inventor in their own right. I read it in one frenzied sitting.'

– Billy-Ray Belcourt, author of *A Minor Chorus*

'The poems of *Slows: Twice* collect in resonance, contemplate the construction of selves, with modes of repetition, sequencing, and mirroring, the way language assembles an identity or points to itself as it points away. "The clouds // disappear the sky sometimes; or they become it." Storied and cubistic, palindromic and cleaved, Liem's poems reveal relationships to time, noise, and duration, and the possibility of joy given painful pasts.'

– Hoa Nguyen, author of *A Thousand Times You Lose Your Treasure*

'"For everything I was, I am now something else." Revision of self and world are core to this innovative, unruly book that manages somehow to be at once formally wacky and emotionally clear. These poems seem to ask: if language is a box heavy with histories and inadequacies and which we nevertheless must carry, can language also carry us somewhere, elsewhere, strangely? Rarely have I encountered a book so at home in the unresolved, in the tension between a longing for declaration and a commitment to questions. T. Liem's work conjures the figure of Janus: god of duality and gates, one face facing an end, the other looking through a new door, right in the eye of a dream.'

– Chen Chen, author of *Your Emergency Contact*
Has Experienced an Emergency

'It's breathtaking to watch words drip from a page into a silver river cutting through a canyon of time. T. Liem sculpts poetry with steady, curious fingers, pushing against the filaments we think hold us together that have been quietly collecting cracks, from buried violence and whispered histories to the fragile connections tying us together. *Obits.* captured my heart; *Slows: Twice* now affirms it.'

    – Teta, founder of diasporic Indonesian publication *Buah zine*

'T. Liem's *Slows: Twice* is a fascinating exercise in revision and remaking, each repetition of its text accomplishing the arduous task of stretching time and geopolitical fixity. "asking and repeating / we are made" declares Liem, and that utterance produces the book's essential maxim, "language is change / changed by prosody." In between these cracks of time, language becomes a miracle suture for love and connection where the hard reality of one's circumstances may produce infinite ruptures. This is a book that peers into the fissure, holding these moments of fracture as still and clearly as possible – a future of proximates.'

    – Muriel Leung, author of *Imagine Us, the Swarm*

SLOWS: TWICE

T. LIEM

COACH HOUSE BOOKS, TORONTO

first edition

Published with the generous assistance of the Canada Council for the Arts and the
Ontario Arts Council. Coach House Books also acknowledges the support of the
Government of Canada through the Canada Book Fund and the Government of Ontario
through the Ontario Book Publishing Tax Credit.

LIBRARY AND ARCHIVES CANADA CATALOGUING IN PUBLICATION

Title: Slows : twice / by T. Liem.
Names: Liem, Tess, author.
Description: Poems.
Identifiers: Canadiana (print) 20220465665 | Canadiana (ebook) 20220465843 | ISBN
9781552454619 (softcover) | ISBN 9781770567559 (EPUB) | ISBN 9781770567566
(PDF)
Classification: LCC PS8623.I363 S56 2023 | DDC C811/.6—dc23

Slows: Twice is available as an ebook: ISBN 978 1 77056 755 9 (EPUB), ISBN 978 1
77056 756 6 (PDF)

Purchase of the print version of this book entitles you to a free digital copy. To claim
your ebook of this title, please email sales@chbooks.com with proof of purchase. (Coach
House Books reserves the right to terminate the free digital download offer at any time.)

'Time is the same from place to place,' I said unfeelingly.
'There is only the eternal present, and biology.'
– Maxine Hong Kingston, *The Woman Warrior*

Often we are forced to consent to the supposition that we are
as continuous as others imagine us to be.
– Erica Hunt, *Jump the Clock*

TABLE OF CONTENTS

I WANT TO LIVE HERE
WHERE NOTHING COHERES

which might incite a utopia

      in which I will not remember

            I wasn't awake in my life.

                  Blood circulated but I was still

          amplifying softness to mimic intimacies.

      Everything sounded

like a shore at night. A threshold

between me and potential in any direction.

Spooked, I revealed myself

in every mirror. I looked down though

the moon appeared to float. I was a yes man

and grabbed whole what was in my reach.

I was outside myself and under tow.

The opposite of eternity

dressed me. It is why I was comfortable

alone, but was I ever really a swimmer.

In my chosen height I was a head above

thought. I was energized by adulthood

but didn't ask what kind of water is this.

It is obviously convenient to have a standard time. A traveller would in setting minutes and seconds remaining the same as at Greenwich. For similar reasons the next best is obviously whole hours in advance or preference to any lesser fraction of the hour, to which his watch have only the hour. Taiping is situated 100° 45' or 6 hours half hour or even quarter hour Kuala Lumpur works out. Kuala Lumpur is situated about 10 6 hours and 43 minutes east of Greenwich. not sure of the exact longitude of Kuala Lumpur about 101° 50' or 6 hours 47 minutes and 20 seconds east Why not therefore adopt the mean of Kuala Lumpur). the mean (approx.) or the 6 ¾ hours meridian 101° 15' east of Greenwich as standard time for the Federated Malay States. A stranger coming to the place and asking Standard time, the reply is given in all round figures 6 ¾ hours before Greenwich, he alters his watch accordingly without interfering with the seconds hand.

1985 –

Days exceed us, ribs stretch skin. Or maybe
that's just me saying if you're lonely, haul someone
else out of yourself. Is asking to be unbodied asking
to ascend or asking to be cast in bronze? My father
transcribed and footnoted his mother's
handwritten autobiography from the year
I was born. Note 46: *In Indonesian the organ
that suffers the pain is liver* [sic] as opposed
to the heart. We need concepts more
than they need us so try again without me
and the grandmother. It's been done.
So take my liver. My colour will not change
suddenly. I will not spill over the edge
of the page when I die. No one wants to field
the question: are metaphors just another power
dynamic between what's described
and what describes it? I mean who—
The rest are reminders. The unloved asked
to contain the loved. (The expressed the un-
expressed.) And I could commit
the rest of life to composing
elements into this dilemma. I could.

A REQUEST

Fix me to your idea of midnight. Meaning
I'm here if you need me. Tomorrow let's spill
water and let our socks sop it up
as we dance. Other things will be true
by then too. Cutting onions with our eyes closed,
humming to the fridge humming: these are the ways
we will exercise faith. No worry if our
wants want nothing to do with us, we will
sharpen our needs.   Say *precise.*
Or is it possible we must ask for things because
we believe, ultimately, in listening?
Sixteen years ago you called me and talked about
the future in a way that scared the shit out of me.
Say *perish the thought.*   How does one do that?
Time aside, the past toppled you unperfect is too close
to say it was. Or tomorrow was a lion's mouth
you would step into.   Meaning
                      ask something of me.
Like the second hand of a clock, if you hear it you
only hear it.   Say *parrot the thought.*
Somewhere I have a picture of a man hidden
behind a picture of a cave.   Say *prick.*
The technical term for this is *etymology.* He was there
meaning something and then he wasn't, meaning slightly
something else.   Say *pressure.*
Somewhere else a slow metronome tocks
another lopsided thought. The somewhere is in the mind,
by which I mean my mind
and with each long sway   say *continue.*
Suppose that was all I said.
If I decided for you too—where are you right now
—say *continue.* We must.

WE WERE CAPTIONED
NOT CAPTURED

I hide in my own shimmering while S. holds a plant
and their camera. On an it's-not-the-heat-it's-the-
humidity kind of day we slugged ourselves to Jean-
Talon Market to buy herbs and succulents. I remember
myself as a crystalline lens swooning light.
                              Ready or not, here I rest.
Exchanging nothing for nothing halts our intention
to buy. We leave hangry. They ask me *what'd you wince*
through to arrive here already obliterated? Except that's
not what they said. I want them to know I am not a
tide. Except I can't afford a property big enough to
hold all the ways I've changed. I didn't wince—my
myths were more casual than that. You couldn't pay
me too much for the details of my first kiss. Then two
ID photos of myself expired and renewed:
                              the subject of a third photo.
The caption: does this haircut make me look gay
enough? I tell them I left the prairies folded up; they
were and weren't home and yet I would return. The
iris of my eye was always itchy, making wanting seem
like darkness stitched to other darkness.

ONE OF THE ONLY PLACES
LEFT UNCROWDED

The screech of a garbage truck left me
in a sleep where I am held
by the same thing that gnaws me. When I said
I was still clamouring in the first draft
of my life, I meant everything I trash
will soon have me needled and pinned.
Tomorrow feels like it could be not-haunted
but so far it never isn't. Months ago I saw someone
carrying a tote bag that said *be courageous,*
it's one of the only places left uncrowded
but why not just say most of us are scared.
Put your arms around me and say it.
Me and my trash, we're warped
through a world that needs neither of us.
We proposed ourselves temporary,
a town of throwaways, but we didn't find
a way out of being thrown. Me and my trash,
we like to think we're good. We're growing
into a kind of crowd wanting
the way the wind scratches us to be the future
shedding itself of our longing.

$1 PER WORD
FOR TRAVEL WRITING

for Liem Sioe Siet

On the first day of the Year of the Pig
my uncle said we would go to the mall
to buy something without saying what.
In the harshly pleasant air-conditioned air
we ate rou song buns and saw young girls staged
in a beauty pageant. I searched
for the word. My uncle pointed, said *meat bread.*
We took in the mall like a centuries-old monument,
escalating and pausing to look down
from each level. Outside heat
waved off the pavement saying *in order*
for a place like this to thrive on hospitality
it must be inhospitable to all activities
other than being hospitable to you. And sometimes
it looked like tourists were sleeping
on every double bed in the country. Less so
in the mall. Stuff another meat bun in my mouth.
In the far-away-from-Here mall it was just like Here
except my prefixed half wasn't worth a dollar. I go on
trying to claim what will not claim me. Identity's
a bit that way, isn't it. Language one barrier—
half travels roughly back to me as not—
skin another. Here where I was raised and born
a stranger stopped me in the street to tell me
in the future everyone would look like me and I take that
to mean my complexion didn't scare him
to his core. Let me swallow another meat song
and sing for you the story of an elementary
school teacher who put her arm next to mine

and told me I wasn't pink like her. In the mall,
my uncle and I, we fulfilled our purpose
of buying common dish soap, and I have a video of him
tossing the bags of liquid into a shopping cart, right
before he raised his arm and said *please,*
take anything you want.

SLOW
MIRROR

between

                                          [you]

          me   &

                                        let   us   slow

&   l   o   w
let us enjoy our own images as an accumulationofwealth

days   o w e d   like dollars   upon owed days

(a g a i n again a   g   a   i   n)

    o n l y up

              each   d   a   y

a gain

a   d   e   b   t

              now   a g a   in   a g a   i n a
gain again a   gain   a g a i n

– 18 –

A THOUSAND
TWANGLING INSTRUMENTS

Listen. I too live with lows. Some last two minutes some two decades. And others. Well. Some make a pretty sentence. Some petty. Some play what you might call a pivotal role. Some are teachers though some teachers aren't meant to be teachers. Some collide with you like a car horn. Some leave you like sweat leaves your skin. Some might say they make you you and whisper blame from bone to bone. Some perennial yet still somehow painful, still somehow new. Though we didn't agree on what was painful, what was new. All this constant, muffled noise. The cement truck whir. The piano upstairs. The spasms of my guts. I have doubled over asking for something new. It's strange to love what can unfold from hurt, to love the din of its ink. But I do and I don't regret pain because it will continue. I don't continue because of pain. For every thing I am, I am also not. For everything I was, I am now something else. I no longer know if these facts are painful. When I say I live with lows, I mean the kind of noise like a neighbour's voice, plump senseless against a wall; or like a bird flunking into a window announcing another season returning.

IN RESPONSE TO FEELING ALONE;
OR, BEFORE AND AFTER

> *Doubtless our lives are solitary but also the inverse.*
> – Jenny Xie

Everything's been known before us OK. The clouds

disappear the sky sometimes; or they become it. When
we stood on Seminyak Beach like a pair of exclamation

points, we heard the same offing tone heard when
someone went to look for their father's corpse in '65

didn't we. After the fact, a siren see-sawed by my open
window more than once. Passing on the street

a voice also said *no I'm alone now* into a phone so it's
possible ghosts also vacation from what's-to-come. How

many people can you name who want to be loved
without enthusiastically loving back? The common cause

of disappearances costs us. We live in the aftermath. In
other words, if one more person tells me

the country of my father's birth is cheap
I will lose it. In other words

this is the only language I speak. To my slightest
disappointment: I'm just writing to say hello. No need

to write back. Don't get me wrong, I want you to want to
know the end of the story, but spoiler alert

you already know they didn't find him; or they found
him a thousand times a thousand times. In other words,

there is always a before and an after tripping over each
other, and if you think an apocalypse

will eliminate the wealth gap, let us hold together the
premonition it will not. Admiration turned me into a

housefly, repeating my body against a window, trying to
get out. I lied low about letting particular men touch me,

but don't leave me now before I recover. Their spines
turned in on the shelves reveal thick wads of time I spent

in omission. Gentle paper, I ask for it back. Doubtless
this moment is our opening.

SOMEONE ASKS
HOW HAVE YOU BEEN

There. There is. There is a. There is a lyric. There is a lyric I. There is a lyric I forget. There is a lyric I forget where. There is a lyric I forget where the. There is a lyric I forget where the phrase. There is a lyric I forget where the phrase is. There is a lyric I forget where the phrase is repeated. There is a lyric I forget where the phrase is repeated like. There is a lyric I forget where the phrase is repeated like this: There is a lyric I forget where the phrase is repeated like this: each. There is a lyric I forget where the phrase is repeated like this: each iteration. There is a lyric I forget where the phrase is repeated like this: each iteration adds. There is a lyric I forget where the phrase is repeated like this: each iteration adds one. There is a lyric I forget where the phrase is repeated like this: each iteration adds one more. There is a lyric I forget where the phrase is repeated like this: each iteration adds one more word. There is a lyric I forget where the phrase is repeated like this: each iteration adds one more word until. There is a lyric I forget where the phrase is repeated like this: each iteration adds one more word until the. There is a lyric I forget where the phrase is repeated like this: each iteration adds one more word until the thought. There is a lyric I forget where the phrase is repeated like this: each iteration adds one more word until the thought has. There is a lyric I forget where the phrase is repeated like this: each iteration adds one more word until the thought has accumulated. There is a lyric I forget where the phrase is repeated like this: each iteration adds one more word until the thought has accumulated itself singing.

A date is a common understanding of a not common
experience

A date is a common understanding of a
common experience

A date is a not common understanding of a
common experience

A date is a not common understanding of a not
common experience

THE MIDDLE OF NOWHERE
IS SOMEWHERE

I don't sleep in the Motel 6
from a dream in which
as a highway
ground to sky
on the other side of a wall
on the other side of a phone
night of her life
The town we're in smells but
Because we notice
it must be blood
being pulled out inside
We're in the province
and there hasn't been enough
away from fires
I like telling people
they don't ask like Lynn
Her eyes looked wet
her son's crops had to be
to get insurance money
how farmers got two dollars
for cattle this year
she knew it
it was nice to be
We sighed and she said
In less than two hours the sun
only through clouds
the rays look almost like rain
toward the illusion
only my mind travels in
The stripe of light curling along
like a border

or rather I'm pulled
the voice I saw
being stretched from
becomes a woman's
She is telling someone
she is having the worst
stuck at the Motel 6
everywhere has a smell
we speculate
The insides of animals
this slaughterhouse city
where I grew up
rain and we've driven
toward other fires
where I'm from when
at the tourist centre
when she told us how
cut down
for the loss
less per pound
When I named my town
and I can't lie
so specific
well I'll let you go
will direct itself
in such a way
We'll be driving
But at the Motel 6
the early morning dark
the hem of the curtain
reminds me

I am
Names Nations and Prepositions
sends me to a movie
Planes, Trains and Automobiles
I don't remember one scene
of the plot include
and one is having the worst
which might've meant
of having missed a flight
comic relief
I am here because of desire
the relief
and myself
But we won't be in any movie
we wouldn't recognize each
face to face
Everyone's worst night
Someone's nowhere is
Forgive me the detour
like I am who I say I am
of leaving
of the kind of words
right at you
in the middle of nowhere
When we hear an engine
has arrived
like she asked
open or close
she got to leave
like days

a collection of
and this rhythm
I watched as a kid
Beyond its title
but the bones
two white men
few days of his life
the inconvenience
The other man
and a ride somewhere
as I wish I could be
and the ride home
and a stranger
the woman and me
other if we were
in the broadest daylight
is someone else's night
someone else's middle
as I don't always feel
I've been on either side
I've been on either side
that look
and leave you

we know someone
to take her
but we don't hear a door
so we can only guess
like nights
like hour after hour

ADVICE

Even while he spoke the words, we were moving on.
– Dante

Ask only what the fortune teller asks and let
hours appoint signs and symbols.
When predictions arrive intact, you might weep

for their talent. In the great ditch, Virgil said pity was not
appropriate for the seers were defrauders
and their purpose, blasphemous.

It is hard to look back. That's easy punishment.
Harder to face what looks back at you. What
twisting could hold us, what warning—

EVEN EARLIER
TODAY IS PAST

Earlier I went to the grocery store hungry and couldn't
                                        hold back.
Three heads of garlic stacked in purple mesh, spots of rot
on red potatoes, green tinted bananas, fluorescence,
                        there was nothing I didn't reach for.
                        You must know what that's like.
This time yesterday, I binged a song
about the sun on repeat, swallowing the kind of
aloneness that quiets you
                        the way snow melts into an eyelash.
                        It was the day before a snowstorm.
It was the day before today. I checked the weather,
knew what to expect even though I admit
I forgot about the forecast
                                until this morning, in it.
This is one way I have known joy:
                the sky feathering down like it said it would.
This time yesterday, I wasn't hungry
because I sat on the floor
                        tearing bread, dipping it in spiced yogourt,
using the area rug as a napkin.
The pattern is made up of heavy reds and blues.
                        I think it's called forgiving.
Let me be the snow, predictable, cool against the cheek.
Lately my stomach pits itself against me,
                        but I still eat and reach and eat.
Lately I've been angry at myself and others,
                        but I still love.

As I walked home,
hunger seemed to have something
in common with joy. How it can lift you again and again

                                        to pick up everything you can carry.
                                    I did not feel joyful. I felt joyful.
I couldn't decide. My arms were tired.
Don't ask me what else I dragged home
hanging off my body

                                        though there is more.
                                        There is always more.

POEM IN WHICH I AM THE LILY
AND THE VALLEY

Lilies-of-the-valley nod[1]

when their fathers ask *how are you?*[2]

saya tidak mengerti sayang selamat pagi sayang
apa kabar sayang baik sayang kasih sayang sayang[3]

I don't understand dear good morning dear what news
dear good thank you my dear[4]

There will be a point at which you will have to let
what you've made of yourself rest

as a bloom so heavy it releases a new way to please[5]

Nod hello nod goodbye[6]

In every surface, survey your features[7]

I chalked up my existence to love
and geopolitical circumstances

CONSIDER THE HANDS
YOU WILL NOT TOUCH

Quiet your mind. Hard work and luck surround you. Take a shower before you make a big decision. What an older sister said about our bodies sagging was right, but she was wrong about when, how, why. Like how the word *hunger* remembers itself in every language no matter how you chew it. Season your skillet properly is all I ask. The last lie you told doesn't count because when you said it, you wished it were true. To wash plastic before you recycle it is a standard way to consider the hands you will not touch. Time is also a standard. The boy who declared the worst thing about you was something a man had done to you—tell him you loved him for a time too. Inside another book is one mother's anger so fluid with her sadness it is nearly a puddle you can see yourself in. Inside another apartment is the phrase *natural light*. Inside another sink is nothing. Your losses return to you like a hammer to a string. There is this sour ache in the archive of your lower intestine. You want to know what happens next and you will. Sometimes you'll know before it happens. Have you seen what people are doing to live? The longest part of your life is still calling for an image.

sʋn

Ɯɐʎqǝ

Ɯɐʎqǝ

THE PAST

THE PAST

Maybe

Maybe

sun

Maybe

one of two.

Maybe

singing

Maybe

warning. Maybe

collapse   toward it.
    Maybe

                                    not

                        Maybe

            Maybe

                            Maybe
                                            both

THERE ARE NO ACTUAL MONSTERS
IN THIS POEM I HOPE

Stitches in her chin, bikes abandoned
at the bottom of a hill, only sky behind us.

I'm still oozing out looking at her
saying *I love you.*

I didn't say it then, but I say it now.

Also known as being fashionably late.

Walking up, we cupped our hands under her chin, taking
care to save the street from being stained.

Also known as protecting what hurt us.

Downhill, we were thrilled by the laws of gravity
pulling us. She coasted until a pothole threw her.

To say what it meant would be deceptive, but I've done
it, citing the time we kissed as the first sign

of something that might burst open
if never spoken, and I'll do it again.

At the time we didn't have the words to chew through.
Like a mouth, language can be bite, lick, and kiss.

We ate the kind of candy made pretty with carnauba
wax. We sat under a desk

playing a game we called *party*,
It was day and we were alone.

Decades pass and I wake with a sandpaper tongue,
wondering if it was just me

under the desk
drooling.

Have you ever picked at your past until
it's all drip and shine?

Just me?

I've been keeping a list of the ways I am monstrous.
Let me tell you how it ends:

On a hill. Slow mouth full

SLOW
MIRROR

every   fumbled

              word
                                          a   w o r s h i p

like

        rain

                   d e d i c a t e d

     to surface

                                               &
e v a p o r a t i n g

o n e i m a g e p r e s s i n g i t s e l f a g a inagainstitself

ONLY ONCE IN THIS LIFETIME
WERE YOU THE BUR OAK

When you want to be one of the bur oaks in the open field of Jarry Park, you think about other things too, but most of the time you think about the bur oak. The yellow-green cling of its bark. How time would merely ring inside you. It's a specific bur oak, but you also often think about how many bur oaks there are in the world and the number is unfathomable. This is very tiring. It took hundreds of years for you to connect your exhaustion with how much you think about the bur oak. When you think about bur oaks now, you try to stop. If you look up, there might be a clothesline pinned with socks from end to end, or someone looking out a window. There might be a question you remember to ask your mother. You might get to jump into the cold water of a lake or see your tall brother waving on the other side of automatic doors at the airport. From time to time there is a glowing ache in your thighs as you pedal a bicycle. This steals your attention from the bur oak. Occasionally you sleep. Your dreams are nearly indistinguishable and only once in this lifetime have you appeared as the bur oak. Once or twice you have even stayed up all night falling in love with a person and forgotten the bur oak completely. You've been told it is quite common. A lot of people want to be a bur oak. Sometimes this makes you cry and you sit down to cry. Crying is not a standing thing. How does anyone cry unfolded like that? Perhaps this is why you want to be the bur oak, always standing, and not the weeping willow, which is altogether too obvious a choice, not that anyone really chooses to want this.

THE SECOND HALF
FOLDS IN ON ITSELF

asking and repeating
we are made

it is a learning process
to drape tenderness around our questions

I don't claim
to be unique

allegiance to place is
a mirror in which
you make eye contact
with a stranger

language is change
changed by prosody

later an offer
a translation

unplanned, a wood rat is born with rising intonation
do you speak any other languages?

lexicon of what I call myself
coincides with lexicon
of what I have been called

in the same century
the provincial rat program is declared a success
I conceive of what a border could consist of
(an image calls for its life)

apa Bahasa lain yank amu kusai

a father and mother meet
one nation after another

there is no place and time
without names

each word is a drawer

in a black and white photo
waterfalls stripe
a background or a border
between grandmother and
                    grandfather

their bodies become an etymology

in lingua rubiginosa nos

I was called tikus
I was called rat
as a term of endearment

I was a living language

the reflection imperfected

the past becomes an exercise where I draw
in the negative space

another grandmother stands resting
her hand on a chair with no one in it

Begin anywhere
Begin

Begin
Begin anywhere

her hand on a chair with no one in it
another grandmother stands resting

in the negative space
the past becomes an exercise where I draw

the reflection imperfected

I was a language living

in terms of year
I was rat
I was tikus

in lingua rubiginosa nos

our bodies become an etymology

grandfather
between grandmother and
a background or a border
waterfalls stripe
black and white

each word is a drawer

without names
there is no place and time

one nation after another
a father and mother meet

apa Bahasa lain yank amu kusai

an image calls 3 1 0-RATS
to conceive of what a border couldn't hold out
it is a success to see yourself
in another century

lexicon of what I has been called
coincides with
lexicon of what I calls self

are you good at any other languages?
unplanned, a wood rat is born with rising intonation

a translation
is a late offer

craned by proximity
language is a crane

with a stranger
you make
a mirror
a place

to be unique
I (ex)claims

to drape tenderness around questions
it is a leaning process

we are made
asking and repeating

When will you arrive? Do you want to be a large gross fruit? Were you trained to think of the choices you did not make? But do you think under everything like a rot? Were you a sun engorged by green? And how did time reason inside? Was it something particular in the world, a number or a vast gift that gave you vertigo? Was it very shiny, very told? Were there a hundred years doing you in? In between that shining sound that rings when you think and now, when did the chance arrive? When will you try less for longer to be a large gross fruit? If you liven your sight, maybe there is a chorus of lows attending to all this longness all the time. Could you see it from the window? What is the question you want to pose for your mirror? In the future will you chance the cold water of a body? What will you see waving from the other side of automatic? Of time of time when the lows diffuse days, will you rest your legs? If you were a large gross fruit would it hurt less to think? Does some time sleep? Are your dreams always memories? You were not only you once in your life were you? Was it once or twice you fell for night? Who let you forget the gross fruit? Tell me, were you ever a currant? Well you, like many, have been the gross fruit. Does that make you plural? What else can you stand? How does anyone stand being gross like that? What seems obvious is hoping, full volume, to be waved forward, to be waves.

every   fumbled

                    word

a   worship

                              like

                    rain

dedicated

                    to surface

&

          evaporating

oneimagepressingitselfagainstitself

THERE WERE NO ACTUAL POETS
IN THIS POEM I HOPE

Full mouth tell me slow

when I'm over   Ending how a hill ends
Monstrous as a list of the ways you've kept

me just
I am the poem dripping shiny   Picked and

drooling
A desert under me

wonders was there
sand against your tongue   Decay passes

through days like this   Alone
one part of you plays itself in a game

I am you made of wax
We are two of a kind

The way words will suck you in   Same
I'm in your jaw sore from gnawing at meaning

Again is my favourite demand
Something opens when I burst

into time   Lip pressed lips
I'd be lying if I said I wasn't

trying to pull us through pain
that defies the syntactic laws of earlier and later

I don't know what will protect you

from turning a street to stained glass
or what will carry you through what hurt you

Revise me as the poem of belated apology
lifting and lilting some unsaid

you   You saying *I love*
pointing at the sunset with your chin

if she arrived like the sun

Maybe if she wore another outfit,
a flowy floral print, a little skin. Maybe
dramatic. Maybe if she wore another outfit,
Maybe if she did not scream so shrill. If she were not so sorrowful, so

THE PAST

THE PAST

Maybe if she did not scream so shrill. If she were not so sorrowful, so
dramatic. Maybe if she wore another outfit,
a flowy floral print, a little skin. Maybe

if she arrived like the sun, which is to say not arrive at
all, but let the movement of her past reveal her each
morning. Maybe if a choice other than one of two.

Maybe if she walked next to the horse, if the horse did
not gallop, if she were alone and singing to herself.
Maybe if she used reverse psychology. Maybe

if she showed up the day before, giving one night to
sleep on her warning. Maybe if she showed up as an
omen. Bring back the horse, but have it

collapse so the past might run toward it.
Maybe if she appeared content, only showing subtle
signs of dissatisfaction, not explaining outright

the disappointment. Maybe if she prepared a Power
Point presentation ~~with proper research and credible
sources like a father. Maybe if she were less~~

~~enigmatically bizarre. Maybe if she appeared more
objective. Her family home seemed to be both at the top
and the bottom of the hill so there was nowhere to run
except toward it, twisted with vision.~~

One tenth of a second was invented over one hundred years ago and it
wasn't the shortest duration to be hammered to life. Not for long. Long
as a lower intestine, you'll live you'll see. A coincidence will string you
together. Gut the archives to find out what happens next. Lift the lid of
an apartment piano and see how repeating touch becomes song. There
is nothing inside sinking. Inside yourself another. We are filled with
ellipses and reversals and we love them in time too. Often I want to skip
to the end. Often I don't do what I want. To appear consistent someone
must seem true and vice versa. The worst thing about this is we tend to
believe it and we true to what we tend. *Tender* another word for money.
Money another for time since before the tenth of a second. There is a
skill for every sentence no matter how its weather chews you. In every
season hunger senses. This is when and how a sag in time can become a
mind, but not why. There was a beginning with advice, but it is hard
work trying to be lucky. I forget more than I remember and though we
are sometimes quieted from each other consider we are surrounded.

I was born
Of hyphen of slash of sum

Of sun of sun of sun
Hours hours hours

[1] Lily-of-the-valley can live up to ten years, which seems both like a very long time and no time at all.

[2] Lily-of-the-valley is said to be aggressive and invasive. This can be true in a bad location but it is extremely valuable where nothing else grows.

[3] Lily-of-the-valley is not from North America but can thrive in an inner citation.

[4] Lily-of-the-valley should be planted in a relatively sheltered life.

[5] Lily-of-the-valley blossoms sometimes give way to red-orange resembling mosquito bites itched, breaking irritated skin.

[6] Lily-of-the-valley is also subject to style; the hyphens that connect each part of the word are everywhere.

[7] Lily-of-the-valley is not a true species of lily, but it is a member of the lily family.

THOUGH THERE IS MORE
THERE IS ALWAYS MORE

making (it) could mean you find yourself in a grocery store a meal for general consumption

hours of work dissolved into an instant like a slurred word

torn open to reveal a brick of wavy noodles or a sound reflecting

a mixed metaphor known as cheap you find yourselves

saying if you can't get out get versions stacked on versions becoming a duration too long to measure

even in the wrong aisle you and yours are more than plenty and enough

It's tempting to believe in punishment. To believe
a previous life, a wrong done, set you up for this. Your
hand bones prime with pain each morning,

memory making ditches of days. It's tempting
to believe everyone deserves what's coming to them
but don't. That's no way to live. It is hard to look back

at who you were in this life already. And anyway
what pleasure the room silence makes for the ringing
in your ears, to be mortified by who you once were!

My upstairs neighbours
and I don't sleep
on the other side
If heaven exists I pray to god
furniture around at night
under pleasure
but you
a contract that stipulates
I conceive of as a result
belongs to the job
because even now
work is on my mind
while they hollow
Every O
intellectual property
the proud owner of whatever
as a result
of your pleasure
Winded lung
I'm always awake
that is also a floor
I looked up to told me I could
he was referring to
buy and I chose
though the real craving was
and repeated
mouth
unlike the other vowels yet
as to need copyright
Their creative endeavours

are edging every night
until their final O
of the ceiling
please stop bumping
steady as a heartbeat
I haven't told anyone
recently I signed
anything
of the job
Maybe even this
in the sexed-up night
owning me
out the air
they make their own
and now you too are
your mind hears
You are the boss
Lemon-stung tongue
Sometimes it feels like
under a ceiling
When someone
have anything
what his money could
pineapple moon cakes
to be overheard
out of someone else's
O of the throat
not so unique
or permission
jerk out dreams

of small earthquakes distant
vibrating between skull
Have you ever reached out
in the dark
with it?
my problem
is to be irreducible but I spit
syllable on syll— like a pump
cold slow gloam
sunken flecks of desire
and meant them
we're connected
you're the neighbours
and the light fixture
That like these awful
you have been heard
—this is yours

volcanic eruptions
and brain like headlines
to touch something
so you don't collide
That might be
The goal I edge toward
out syllable upon
in a mall fountain
copper nickel coins
I've said many words
As a result
Imagine
the floorboards
shaking out a missive
joyous nights
and repeated

Yours,
        t.

4:00 4:01 4:02 4:03 4:04

4:05 4:06 4:07 4:08 4:09

4:10 4:11 4:12 4:13 4:14

4:15 4:16 4:17 4:18 4:19

4:20 4:21 4:22 4:23 4:24

4:25 4:26 4:27 4:28 4:29

Time lets you be in the world in so many ways: at 4:02
at 4:03   again again again

4:30 4:31 4:32 4:33 4:34

4:35 4:36 4:37 4:38 4:39

4:40 4:41 4:42 4:43 4:44

4:45 4:46 4:47 4:48 4:49

4:50 4:51 4:52 4:53 4:54

4:55 4:56 4:57 4:58 4:59

There is a lyric I forget where the phrase is repeated like this: each iteration adds one more word until the thought has accumulated itself singing. There is a lyric I forget where the phrase is repeated like this: each iteration adds one more word until the thought has accumulated itself. There is a lyric I forget where the phrase is repeated like this: each iteration adds one more word until the thought has accumulated. There is a lyric I forget where the phrase is repeated like this: each iteration adds one more word until the thought has. There is a lyric I forget where the phrase is repeated like this: each iteration adds one more word until the thought. There is a lyric I forget where the phrase is repeated like this: each iteration adds one more word until the. There is a lyric I forget where the phrase is repeated like this: each iteration adds one more word until. There is a lyric I forget where the phrase is repeated like this: each iteration adds one more word. There is a lyric I forget where the phrase is repeated like this: each iteration adds one more. There is a lyric I forget where the phrase is repeated like this: each iteration adds one. There is a lyric I forget where the phrase is repeated like this: each iteration adds. There is a lyric I forget where the phrase is repeated like this: each iteration. There is a lyric I forget where the phrase is repeated like this: each. There is a lyric I forget where the phrase is repeated like this: There is a lyric I forget where the phrase is repeated like. There is a lyric I forget where the phrase is repeated. There is a lyric I forget where the phrase is. There is a lyric I forget where the phrase. There is a lyric I forget where the. There is a lyric I forget where. There is a lyric I forget. There is a lyric I. There is a lyric. There is a. There is. There.

IN RESPONSE TO FEELING ALONE;
OR, BEFORE AND AFTER

I've been OK before   The present

disappears the past sometimes and then becomes it
Where I stood out

there was neither sand nor exclamation
but the sky was endless   It was the same

prairie town in which I didn't   The way
two things can be true at once   After and before

share a border   Between then and now someone went
to look up what happened in '65

and was distracted by being alone
so it's possible

common knowledge isn't common
About that year Njoo Ay Nio wrote

we have a big problem—only that is a translation
How many languages can you name

that will name you back   After the question
they all step off the see-saw and let me fall ass first

into the unspeakable   On the back of the photo
she signs herself *Nyonya* and

you already know I didn't know what this meant
This is how particularity can multiply or divide

a thousand times a thousand times   In other words
                    we are always talking about the dead

                                     repeating our bodies
                against grief trying to fit itself into what's to come

                    If you think it's just me let us hold together
                                        the premonition

that I is a thing held together   In other words I am
          one of many who can't recognize an open window

                    until it closes   If you get me wrong
          no need to alert authority   Admiration turns

                                        me into fact and
                    every fact has an afterlife

          just like every spine   Time reveals itself
                            like a housefly doubtful

                    the sky was ever cloudless

When the moths come back it's like silence emerging flimsy from the walls, begging. It's like they were never not there. You see exactly one single flyer on a mission each evening since the exterminator came for some other presence that was barely visible and infinite. Like hours, for each one you kill there are countless more you will never meet. For every flight you sway to its end there will be another. All this death pressed hard between the heels of your hands. A prayer in a vise. It must surely hurt you more than anything else. More than them. You only know because you wake up from dreams where you were dust. Like you, the moths continue. Time is senseless against the appearance and disappearance of the moth. Though we did not agree on what kept time and what time keeps. A ball rises in one year and drops in another. Its fall announces something new. Its fall can be painful if you don't feel in any way new. Its fall enacts a collective agreement to something to which we didn't all agree. Most didn't ask for fireworks. Most did not ask for our history the way we must ask for our future. Most didn't ask for midnight to be known by anything other than the sky sweating stars. Well. It's not altogether true. There are places and seasons where night is something else entirely. Look.

SLOW
MIRROR

between

[you]

me   &

let   us   slow

&
l   o   w
let us enjoy our own images as an accumulationofwealth

days o w e d   upon owed days   like dollars   days owed days

(a g a i n again a   g   a   i   n)

o n l y up

each   d   a   y

a gain

a   d   e   b   t

now   aga in   a g a i n a
gain again a gain   a g a i n

ON THE LAST DAYS
OF THE YEAR OF THE OX

We remembered. How the automatic doors
of the mall in Jogjakarta opened like a mouth
and said *parting is such sweet sorrow.*
The joke is cheap but every word
gets me closer to debtless
and I have not been back since
and I have been sorrowful.
More glass, more metal rises
every minute.
If you take anything
from this remember identity isn't sweat
evaporating off your skin.
Though it can dissolve sweet as salt
against the tongue. I'm here as I was there
to be recognized as something,
to link arms with some future
in which I am more than half myself.
In order for a person to be one thing
they can be nothing else
and sometimes it sounds like
a painful song has slept under every tongue.
No amount of time could swallow
such fact. Six o'clock in Jogja felt like
wearing the sky. Like silk. Even
words beautiful enough
to win a pageant couldn't
describe it, no matter their worth.
I couldn't tell you what I tried to say
as a tourist. Stuff another
year in my mouth. Last night

when the sun set in Montreal
it wasn't as harsh as it was
the summer during the fires
not as harsh as it might be again
but the orange of it was so pink
I lost what year it was
what animal was about to depart
which one would return.

Of course there were ways I asked to shed tomorrow
To be timeless   More precisely to be *-less
If you thought of Styrofoam or crowds of plastic bags
Gnawing at ocean water toting them around
No not the time-less-ness of outlasting
Every Monday night I put the trash on the curb and every
Tuesday morning it's taken away and I'm allowed to lessen
Can't you name a few things you'd like less of?
You just need
To look at what you throw away and speak
This schedule of give and take with the curb is a clock
An asterisk could be any thing
n too any number
There are n selves in any self for example
Desire unsolves itself when blood-less brain-less heart-
This is the problem with a tendency toward subtraction
One of the only places left uncrowded
Is a place called wealth
The inhabitants warping themselves away from earth
Wrapping their arms around more plus more
Like the metal jaw of the garbage truck
Yet impervious
To the plentiful work of Tuesday morning
Lessening too can be a form of greed
For n years I've been greedy
Wanting to be y-less
y being something solvable
Tomorrow being itself
Only 'til we sleep and ghost ourselves into it
When I said y was solvable I meant it isn't bad

To be a clamour of need
Though *y* does go on unsolved hour after hour
Though fear scrapes even in sleep
Today could be the day you want all of it anyway

In our   window - free   bedroom
S. stitched   their body to   b e d
phone glow against their gold-green irises
while I itched words against other words
in the dark.   They read out
what a famous bigot said and you couldn't
p a y me enough to repeat it.
W e d i dn't ask for the renewal or expiry
  poems c a n g i v e to s o m e t h i n g
  someone said, some t h i n g that leaves
  you folded like an old photo, but I c a n ' t
  s t o p giving. Does that make me generous?
   In the details you'll n o t i c e   I a m
    the s p e a k e r but not the subject. This is a
     m y t h b i g e n o u g h to h o l d me
     when my bladder is f u l l .   When I peed
     with the door open   while S. cooked
     m u s s e l s,   p r o x i m i t y of bathroom
     to kitchen   meant together it all smelled
     like a beach.   I arrived a t i d e, transported
     by piss. Wouldn't you like to be transported?
     If you had to choose   only   o n e,
     would you go to a time or a place? Slow time,
     speed it up? Either way you'd still have to pee.
     Let me give you a minute. Let me give.
   Let   piss be a   lens for   light.
   One   night S. and I were too s l u g g e d
   to find our way home. We were without time
   or place. In an alley our urine s p l a s h e d
   our ankles but our biggest fear was someone
   would catch us in n e e d, i n s t e a d of

in a bathroom.   Pee was o u r gift
to asphalt, yet we were the grateful ones.
Ready or n o t,
I d o n ' t   always know w h a t to do
with what I have t o o ff e r.   In answer
to my own question, I w o u l d t r a v e l
to   a   year
  in which years   s h i m m e r
relief through our bodies.   S u n b e a m
warm as a kidney.   S u c c u l e n t s
hiding t h r i v i n g roots in d r y s o i l.

Do not fix me   Meaning
that isn't how you need me   Spill tomorrow
across the floor and let it sop us up   Truth is
dancing along with the faith we will find it
whereas I worry I don't ask enough of tomorrow
Even though I have what I need I would like to know
what other kind of living is possible
Last year I saw a woman pressure a man into the street
unbending her arms against him
and it was scary to be unmoved
The bus's brakes were already whistling
Its stop too perfect   to topple him
This gave the scene an air of precision
The technical term for this is *drama*
Meaning
leave me out of it
It was as if she whispered *I didn't really mean it*
He was there and then he was still there
and if you saw him you only saw him
Time aside
There is more I suppose I should say
But it's all lopsided and swaying
as it leaves my mind   and yet I continue
Somewhere else you are something else
The second hand of a clock insists

could I .dilemma ~~this~~ into elements
composing to life ~~of rest the~~
~~commit could~~ I and ~~(.expressed~~
-un the expressed ~~the.) loved the contain~~ to
ask~~ed unloved The. reminders are rest the~~
—who ~~mean I? it~~ describes what ~~and~~
~~described~~ what's between. ~~Dynamic~~
power ~~another just metaphors are: question the~~
~~field to~~ wants ~~one No. die I when. page the of~~
edge ~~the~~ over ~~spill not will I. suddenly~~
change ~~not will colour My .liver my take So~~
~~.done been it's. grandmother the~~ and
~~me without~~ again try ~~so us~~ need ~~they than.~~
more ~~concepts~~ need ~~We. heart the to~~
~~opposed as~~ [sic] ~~liver is pain the suffers that~~
~~organ the Indonesian In: 46 Note. born was I~~
~~year the from autobiography handwritten~~
~~mother's his~~ footnoted and transcribed
~~father My .bronze in~~ cast ~~be to~~ asking ~~or, ascend to~~
asking unbodied ~~be~~ to ask~~ing~~ Is. you~~rself~~ of ~~out else~~
someone ~~haul, lonely~~ You're ~~if saying me just. that's~~
~~maybe Or .skin stretch ribs,~~ us ~~exceed days.~~

... ... d ti... ... 'e h... in ... of ... Greenwich ... t
simplifies calculation. A traveller would in setting his watch have only the hour h... to change the
minutes and seconds remaining the same as at Greenwich.

For similar reasons the next best is obviously half hour or even quarter hour standard time, in
preference to any lesser fraction of the hour, to which Kuala Lumpur works c...

Taiping is situated 100° 45' or 6 hours and 42 minutes east of Greenwich
... Kuala Lumpur is situated about 101° 50' or ... hours 47 minutes and 20 seconds east of Greenwich (I am
... of the exact longitude of Kuala Lumpur)
Why not ... adopt the mean (approx.) of the 6 ¾ hours meridian 101° 15' east of Greenwich as

It is obviously convenient to have a standard time ... e hours in advance of ... Greenwich ... It
simplifies calculation. A traveller would in setting his watch have only the hour h... to change the
minutes and seconds remaining the same as at Greenwich.

For similar reasons the next best is obviously half hour or even quarter hour standard time, in
preference to any lesser fraction of the hour, to which Kuala Lumpur works c...

Taiping is situated 100° 45' or 6 hours and 42 minutes east of Greenwich
... Kuala Lumpur is situated about 101° 50' or ... hours 47 minutes and 20 seconds east of Greenwich (I am
... of the exact longitude of Kuala Lumpur)
Why not ... adopt the mean (approx.) of the 6 ¾ hours meridian 101° 15' east of Greenwich as
standard time for the Federated Malay States.

A stranger coming to the place and asking Standard time the reply is ... 6 ¾
hours before Greenwich, he alters his watch accordingly without interfering with the ... s hand.

... ...
Why not ... adopt the mean (approx.) of the 6 ¾ hours meridian 101° 15' east of Greenwich as
standard time for the Federated Malay States.
A stranger coming to the place and asking Standard time the reply is ... 6 ¾
hours before Greenwich, he alters his watch accordingly without interfering with the ... s hand.

... Kuala Lumpur is situated about 101° 50' or ... hours 47 minutes and 20 seconds east of Greenwich (I am
... of the exact longitude of Kuala Lumpur)
Why not ... adopt the mean (approx.) of the 6 ¾ hours meridian 101° 15' east of Greenwich as
standard time for the Federated Malay States.
A stranger coming to the place and asking Standard time the reply is ... 6 ¾
hours before Greenwich, he alters his watch accordingly without interfering with the ... s hand.

HERE IN
THE FUTURE WE KNOW

Water   was   the   only   kindness

Rest   a dull   thought   above   head

Choice   heightened   I   swam   alone

[and summer was smoke]

Comfort wore a dress   adorned   in   reason

Why   opposed   mortality

Undertow dragged us inside one year   after   another

[and we didn't outside again]

Reaching   a   way   to   be   wholly

Yes   floated   in   the   mirror

Yes   in   every   moon

[and we took it too far]

Spectre of   Yes   revealed   by each   I

Yes   the only direction between then   and now

Night   a shore   threshing   against Yes

[and nights repeated themselves as words]

Everything   was   noise

loud and   proximate to love

Yes   circulating   blood

[and yet]

In   sleep   we remember   the future

[...]

How   we   became   incomprehensible

Poems do end, at least materially.
– Aditi Machado, *The End*

Time to gesture toward what remains.
– Norman Erikson Pasaribu, *Sergius Seeks Bacchus,*
translated from the Indonesian by Tiffany Tsao

SLOWS: TWICE

T. LIEM

NOTES

p. 9: The title 'I Want to Live Here Where Nothing Coheres' is a line from Alice Notley's poem '"I Couldn't Sleep in My Dream"' from *Certain Magical Acts*.

pp. 11/81: The cut-up and erased texts beginning 'It is obviously … ' and the margin text beginning 'On the other hand … ' are from the records of the Proceedings of the Legislative Council of the Straits Settlements for the year 1900, which is the year the British decided Singapore Mean Time would be adopted in the settlements.

p. 12: In '1985 – ' the phrase 'the expressed / the unexpressed' refers to an idea/phrase that came from Maggie Nelson's *The Argonauts*.

pp. 12/69: The Njoo Ay Nio quoted in '1985 – ' and 'In Response to Feeling Alone' is my paternal grandmother.

p. 19: The title 'A Thousand Twangling Instruments' is a line from *The Tempest* by William Shakespeare.

p. 20: The epigraph for 'In Response to Feeling Alone' is from *Eye Level* by Jenny Xie.

pp. 23/67: 'Time You Can't Argue With' is the phrase Agnès Varda used to describe 'objective time' in her film/lecture *Varda by Agnès*.

p. 26: The epigraph for 'Advice' is from 'Canto XX' in *The Inferno of Dante* translated by Robert Pinsky.

pp. 32/58: The poems titled 'The Past' use the episode of *The Twilight Zone* called 'Spur of the Moment' as source material.

p. 51: 310-RATS was the number to call to report a rat, or signs of rats, in Alberta.

p. 54: 'You Were Not One Time in Your Life' is a re-translation/adaptation back into English from a French translation Simon Brown did and shared with me of 'Only Once in This Lifetime Were You the Bur Oak' (p. 37).

p. 62: The text for 'Notes in Which I Am the Lily and the Valley' was taken and adapted from '#YouShouldGrowThis: Lily-of-the-valley is a valuable plant' by Lyndon Penner, published on 16 May 2015 on CBC News.

Versions of some of the poems in this book were first published in the following journals. Thank you to the editors and staff who published this work and provided a space to share and connect.

GUEST
CV2
underblong
The Boston Review
Peach Mag
Maisonneuve
filling Station
Apogee
The Slowdown Podcast
The Fiddlehead
The Malahat Review
Catapult
Ampersand Review

The research and writing of this book were possible because of financial support from the Canada Council for the Arts as well as from the Conseil des arts et des lettres du Québec.

One photo referred to in 'The Second Half Folds in on Itself' is of my maternal grandparents, Richard and Winnifred Knowles, at Niagara Falls sometime in the 1970s.

The other photo referred to is of my paternal grandmother, Njoo Ay Nio.

She had a few different pictures taken of her that year, and on the back of each was a note. The one to me, which is referenced in 'In Response to Feeling Alone; or, Before and After' (p. 69), said this:

untuk Tessa. Liem
foto Oma Maria manило
Njorogino
usia 88 taun   (Njhum Ayio 2)
1-3-1992

Accompanying the scan of this note, my father explained:

Notes (You may already know)

- *untuk = for*
- *Maria Monica = her baptized name (she was the mother of St. Augustine?)*
- *Nyoo Ay Nio (signature: her maiden name)*
- *usia = age*
- *taun (often also spelled tahun) = year(s)*
- *Ny = nyonya = Mrs.*
- *Liem Djie Ie (signature; her husband's name)*

These pictures sit on and above my desk. I wanted to include them so they would be seen and not just referenced in the poem. I also wanted to show the translation that happens in order for me to understand something about them. These materials give me some connection to family, to other places and times, but mostly they remind me that to know about the past I must ask.

ACKNOWLEDGEMENTS

My writing over the past few years was supported by workshops offered by Winter Tangerine, Kasia Van Schaik, Hoa Nguyen, Hedgebrook, and Kundiman. Thank you to the facilitators and participants for making a thoughtful, generous community to write with. Likewise, thank you to the participants in the two workshops I lead—you showed up for me in so many ways, and I'm honoured to have spent time with you.

Thanks, Shazlin Rahman, for gracing this book with your art and for the HerSarong project.

Thanks to everyone at Coach House for your hard work and patience, for transforming the text in my mind into a book. Thanks especially to Jordan Abel, for spending time with these poems and ideas, and helping me see more possibility in all of it—your insights and support have kept me afloat yet immersed.

To those of you who invited me on walks, or to your kitchen table, and to those who were up for video calls to catch up, to talk about poetry or whatever we were reading or not-reading, to just wave *hello*—I'm grateful for the breaks from silence these moments provided.

Thanks to my parents for sharing stories about your parents.

Most of all, thanks to Surah, the S. in the poems, the sunlight warming us, the warmth.

T. Liem was born and raised in Vegreville, Alberta, and now lives in Montreal, Quebec. They are the author of *OBITS.* (2018), which was shortlisted for a Lambda Literary Award and won the Gerald Lampert Memorial Award as well as the A. M. Klein Prize. Their writing has been published in *Catapult, Apogee, Plenitude,* the *Boston Review, Grain, Maisonneuve, Best Canadian Poetry 2018* and *2019,* and elsewhere.

Typeset in Arno and Graphie.

Printed at the Coach House on bpNichol Lane in Toronto, Ontario, on Zephyr Antique
Laid paper, which was manufactured, acid-free, in Saint-Jérôme, Quebec, from second-
growth forests. This book was printed with vegetable-based ink on a 1973 Heidelberg
KORD offset litho press. Its pages were folded on a Baumfolder, gathered by hand, bound
on a Sulby Auto-Minabinda, and trimmed on a Polar single-knife cutter.

Coach House is on the traditional territory of many nations, including the Mississaugas
of the Credit, the Anishnabeg, the Chippewa, the Haudenosaunee, and the Wendat
peoples, this territory is now home to many diverse First Nations, Inuit, and Métis
peoples. We acknowledge that Toronto is covered by Treaty 13 with the Mississaugas
of the Credit. We are grateful to live and work on this land.

Edited for the press by Jordan Abel
Cover design by Crystal Sikma, cover artwork *Golden Eclipse 002* by Shazlin Rahman
Interior design by Crystal Sikma
Author photo by Surah Field-Green

Coach House Books
80 bpNichol Lane
Toronto ON M5S 3J4
Canada

416 979 2217
800 367 6360

mail@chbooks.com
www.chbooks.com